Tina Turner Music Legend 83

|Biography, Achievements, Career, Cause of Death and Facts You Didn't Know About Her|

Martin Herman

All rights reserved. No part of this publication may be reproduced, distributed, or transmitted in any form or by any means, including photocopying, recording, or other electronic or mechanical methods, without the prior written permission of the publisher, except in the case of brief quotations embodied in critical reviews and certain other noncommercial uses permitted by copyright law.

Copyright © Martin Herman, 2023.

Table of Contents

Introduction

Chapter 1: Who was Tina Turner?

Early Life and Adolescence

Career

Relationships and Marriage

Chapter 2: Awards and Achievements

Chapter 3: Facts About Tina Turner You Didn't Know

Introduction

Tina Turner, the spearheading rock'n'roll star who turned into a pop behemoth during the 1980s, has kicked the bucket at age 83 after a long disease.

She had experienced weakness lately, being determined to have gastrointestinal malignant growth in 2016 and having a kidney relocated in 2017.

Turner avowed and enhanced People of color's developmental stake in rock'n'roll, characterizing that period of music to the degree that Mick Jagger owned up to taking motivation from her high-kicking, vivacious live exhibitions for his stage persona. Following twenty years of working with her harmful spouse, Ike Turner, she struck out alone and - after a couple of premature moves - became one of the characterizing pop symbols of the 1980s with the collection Private Artist. Her life was chronicled in three journals, a biopic, a jukebox melodic, and in 2021, the acclaimed narrative film, Tina.

Tina Turner, the 'Sovereign of Rock'n Roll' has kicked the bucket calmly today at 83 years old after a long illness in her home in Kusnacht close to Zurich, Switzerland. With her, the world loses a music legend and a good example.

Turner was conceived by Anna Mae Bullock on 26 November 1939 and brought up in Nutbush, Tennessee, where she picked cotton with her family as a youngster. She sang in the minuscule town's congregation ensemble, and as a teen talked - or rather, sang - her way into Ike's band in

St Louis: he had declined her solicitation to join until he heard her hold onto the receiver during a Rulers of Cadence execution for a version of BB Lord's You Realize I Love You.

She made her recorded presentation under the name with the Ike and Tina Turner single A Dolt in Affection in July 1960, which broke the US Top 30 and began a run of decent outline achievement. Yet, it was their live exhibitions that made them a sensation. Ike visited the Ike and Tina Turner Revue forcefully on the Chitlin' Circuit - remembering in front of integrated crowds, such was their business power. In 1964, they endorsed Warner Brothers engrave Loma Records, which delivered their most memorable collection to diagram: Live! The Ike and Tina Turner Show.

Chapter 1: Who was Tina Turner?

Turner was an incredible vocalist, musician, creator, and entertainer, who is most popular for her strong voice that arrived at the most noteworthy ups and least downs, combined with her vivacious and spellbinding live exhibitions.

Starting her profession during the 1950s, and arriving at notoriety during the 1960s close by her ex, Ike Turner, she made her greatest progress when she started performing solo during the 1980s.

Tina started her profession with Ike Turner's Rulers of Mood in 1957, and first showed up on record under the name Little Ann. Following her split from Ike during the 1970s, she sent off what became known as "perhaps of the best rebound in music history".

Her 1984 multi-platinum collection Private Artist was a success all over the planet, and she immediately became one of the most incredible selling specialists ever.

Tina additionally acted in the movies Tommy, Distraught Max Past Thunderdome and Last Activity Legend, and her 1993 biopic What's Adoration Have to Do with It, carried her story to many more fans.

She sold north of 100 million records, procured 12 Grammy Grants selections, three Grammy Corridor of Popularity grants, and a Grammy Lifetime Accomplishment Grant. She was additionally the main dark craftsman and the primary female to be on the front of Drifter.

Early Life and Adolescence

Tina Turner was born Anna Mae Bullock on 26 November 1939 in the little rustic town of Nutbush, Tennessee. Her dad Floyd dealt with a neighborhood ranch.

She had a disturbed youth. She and her senior sister Aillene were isolated when her folks moved to work in a weapons plant, and the youthful Anna Mae went to live with severely strict grandparents.

At the point when the family were brought together after the conflict, Anna

Mae began singing in a nearby Baptist church.

Her mom left when she was only 11 and, after two years, when her dad remarried, Anna and her sister were shipped off to live with her grandma in Brownsville, Tennessee.

She turned into a team promoter at her neighborhood school, played ball and partook in a feverish public activity. On graduating in 1958, she found a new line of work at an emergency clinic in St Louis, Missouri, and set off to turn into a medical caretaker.

It was in a club, where she and her sister had gone for the night, that she originally saw Ike Turner perform with his band, The Rulers of Musicality.

Career

She made her recorded show under the name with the Ike and Tina Turner single A Nitwit in Veneration in July 1960, which broke the US Top 30 and started a run of decent chart achievement. Yet, it was their live exhibitions that made them a sensation. Ike visited the Ike and Tina Turner Revue forcefully on the Chitlin' Circuit - remembering in front of integrated crowds, such was their business power. In 1964, they endorsed Warner Brothers engrave Loma Records, which delivered their most memorable collection to graph: Live! The Ike and Tina Turner Show.

In the last part of the 60s, the couple were sought by a larger number of people of rock's greatest names. Phil Spector created the 1966 single Waterway Profound - Mountain High;

they upheld the Drifters in the UK and later the US, and stars including David Bowie, Wily Stone, Cher, Elvis Presley and Elton John visited them in their Las Vegas residency.

They were a graph making, Grammy-winning power during the 1970s - a run that reached a conclusion when Turner left Ike, who had been reliably rough and faithless, in 1976. Her last single with the gathering was Child, Get It On, from the 1975 film variation of the Who's rock drama Tommy, where she featured as Corrosive Sovereign, a person of a similar name of her second independent collection.

In the separation, settled in 1978, Turner left with only two vehicles and the freedoms to her stage name. "Ike battled a smidgen since he understood how I would manage it," she said in the narrative Tina.

Turner, who had proactively delivered two performance records kept seeking after a performance profession, however it would take until she delivered her fifth collection, 1984's Confidential Artist, for her to override the old picture of the shimmying rock'n'roller - and get away from untimely transfer to the oldies circuit - with one of a strong, mullet-donning, cowhide clad pop symbol.

In the narrative Tina, she portrayed Private Artist as her presentation. "I don't think of it as a rebound," she said. "Tina had never shown up."

Turner credited Buddhism and especially the act of reciting with emphatically influencing her life during the 1980s. Outside music, she featured in Frantic Max Past Thunderdome opposite Mel Gibson in 1985. She distributed her most memorable diary, the worldwide blockbuster I, Tina, in 1986, which was subsequently adjusted into the 1993 film What's Affection Have to Do With It? featuring Angela Bassett as Turner. In 1995, she sang the subject tune to the James Bond film GoldenEye.

Turner reported her retirement in 2000, a year in the wake of delivering her last independent collection, 24 Seven, however she would get back to the stage in 2008, performing at the Grammy grants with Beyoncé, and for a last visit to stamp 50 years of her vocation.

That was definitely the end. "I was simply burnt out on singing and satisfying everyone," she told the New

York Times in 2019. "That is all I'd at any point finished in my life."

Turner worked together on the melodic Tina with Phyllida Lloyd, which debuted in 2018 and won Laurence Olivier and Tony grants for its separate West End and Broadway runs. "This melody isn't about my fame," Turner said of the creation. "It is about the excursion I took to arrive. Every night I believe crowds should detract from the theater so that you can transform poison into medication."

In 2020, a remix of her 1984 hit What's Adoration Have to Do With It? by the Norwegian maker Kygo made Turner the main craftsman to have a UK Top 40 hit in seven consecutive years. In 2021, she was enlisted into the Wild Lobby of Distinction as an independent craftsman, 30 years after Ike and Tina Turner's enlistment.

Relationships and Marriage

Tina met Ike at an East St. Louis club called Club Manhattan in 1957 when she was still a high schooler. She allegedly played out Ike's adaptation of B.B. Lord's notorious "You Realize I Love You," and they in a flash became companions. Their developing trap, be that as it may, was everything except basic. Ike was still seeing someone who lived with Lorraine Taylor when he started his issue with Tina. Besides, Tina had become pregnant during her senior year of secondary school with saxophonist Raymond Slope from Ike's band Lords of Mood.

The team proceeded to shape the Ike and Tina Turner Revue, delivering hit after R&B hit together. The option of notable reinforcement vocalists/artist The Ikettes simply added to their prevalence. They moved to Los Angeles and supposedly wedded in Tijuana, Mexico, in 1962 — however Ike later disproved the marriage as legitimate, expressing that it was a customary marriage.

Regardless, the marriage went on through 1976, when the unbelievable vocalist at last petitioned for legal separation after a rough episode, referring to "hostile contrasts." The separation was settled in Spring of 1978.

Tina had previously brought forth her most memorable youngster, Craig Slope when her marriage with Ike had started. Ike and Tina had one child together,

Ronnie Turner, in October of 1960, and Tina later embraced Ike's two kids from a past marriage. Thus, Ike embraced Craig, and the couple changed his name to Craig Turner.

Chapter 2: Awards and Achievements

Turner recently held a Guinness World Record for the biggest paying crowd (180,000 of every 1988) for an independent entertainer.

In the UK, Turner was the principal craftsman to have a best 40 hit in seven continuous years; she has a sum of 35 UK top 40 hits. She has sold north of 100 million records around the world, including guaranteed RIAA collection deals of 10 million.

Turner has won a sum of 12 Grammy Grants. These honors incorporate eight serious Grammy Grants; she shares the record (with Pat Benatar) for most honors given for Best Female Stone Vocal Performance.Three of her accounts, "Stream Profound - Mountain High" (1999), "Glad Mary" (2003) and "What's Love Have to Do with It" (2012) are in the Grammy Corridor of Fame.Turner was the main female craftsman to win a pop Grammy, rock and R&B fields. Turner got a Grammy Lifetime Accomplishment Grant in 2018. Turner likewise won Grammys as an individual from USA for Africa and as an entertainer at the 1986 Rulers Trust show.

Turner got a star on the Hollywood Stroll of Notoriety in 1986 and a star on the St. Louis Stroll of Notoriety in 1991. She was enlisted into the Wild Corridor of Distinction as a pair with Ike Turner in 1991.

In 2005, Turner got the renowned Kennedy Community Respects. A few craftsmen honored her that late evening including Melissa Etheridge (performing "Stream Profound - Mountain High"), Sovereign Latifah (playing out "What's Adoration Have to Do with It"), Beyoncé (performing "Glad Mary"), and Al Green (playing out "We should Remain Together").

In 2021, Turner was drafted by Angela Bassett into the Stone and Roll Lobby of Distinction as an independent craftsman. Keith Metropolitan and H.E.R. played out "It's Just Love", Mickey Guyton played out "What's Adoration Have to Do with It", and Christina Aguilera performed "Stream Profound - Mountain High."

Her Awards Follows:

1962

- May 29 - 4th Annual Grammy Awards (USA)

1970

- March 11 - 12th Annual Grammy Awards (USA)

1972

- March 15 - 14th Annual Grammy Awards (USA)

1975

- March 01 - 17th Annual Grammy Awards (USA)

1984

- Bravo Otto (Germany)

1985

- September 13 - MTV Video Music Awards (USA)
- February 26 - 27th Annual Grammy Awards (USA)
- January 28 - American Music Awards (USA)
- CableACE Award (USA)
- Hammerschlumpf (Germany)

- Bravo Otto (Germany)

1986

- December 13 - NAACP Image Awards (USA)
- September 05 - MTV Video Music Awards (USA)
- August 28 - Hollywood Walk of Fame (USA)
- February 25 - 28th Annual Grammy Awards (USA)

1987

- August 27 - Berolina (Germany)
- February 24 - 29th Annual Grammy Awards (USA)

- January 26 - American Music Awards (USA)

1988

- March 02 - 30th Annual Grammy Awards (USA)
- Guinness World Records (Worldwide)

1989

- February 22 - 31th Annual Grammy Awards (USA)
- January 18 - Rock & Roll Hall Of Fame (USA)

1990

- April 12 - Goldene Europa (Germany)
- February 21 - 32th Annual Grammy Awards (USA)

1991

- May 19 - St. Louis Walk of Fame (USA)
- February 20 - 33th Annual Grammy Awards (USA)
- January 16 - Rock & Roll Hall Of Fame (USA)

1992

- February 12 - Goldene Kamera (Germany)

1993

- May 29 - Essence Awards (USA)
- May 13 - World Music Awards (Monaco)
- February 24 - 35th Annual Grammy Awards (USA)

1994

- March 01 - 36th Annual Grammy Awards (USA)

1996

- May 26 - Walk of Fame Europe (Netherlands)
- February 12 - Chevalier Des Arts Et Lettres (France)

1998

- February 25 - 40th Annual Grammy Awards (USA)
- February 14 - NAACP Image Awards (USA)

1999

- November 04 - Premios Amigo (Spain)
- October 07 - MOBO Awards (UK)
- February 24 - Grammy Hall of Fame (USA)

2000

- January 22 - NRJ Music Awards (France)
- January - VTM (Belgium)

-
- Guinness World Records (Worldwide)

2001

- May 20 - Sankt Louis Walk of Fame (USA)

2002

- May 23 - W.C. Handy Blues Awards (USA)
- February 27 - 44th Annual Grammy Awards (USA)

2003

- February 23 - Grammy Hall of Fame (USA)

2004

- April 13 - Memphis Heroes Awards (USA)

2005

- December 04 - Kennedy Center Honors (USA)
- November 03 - Women of the Year Award (UK)
- February 13 - 47th Annual Grammy Awards (USA)
- February 13 - Goldene Kamera Award (Germany)

2007

- February 11 - 49th Annual Grammy Awards (USA)

2008

- February 02 - 50th Annual Grammy Awards (USA)

2009

- May 19 - Live Design Awards (USA)

2010

- January 09 - SwissAward (Switzerland)
- Cyprus Music Awards (Greece)

2011

- Cyprus Music Awards (Greece)

2012

- February 12 - Grammy Hall of Fame (USA)

2014

- October 31 - Tara Award (Thailand)

2018

- October 05 - Grammy Lifetime Achievement (USA)

2021

- October 30 - Rock & Roll Hall Of Fame (USA)

Books
- I, Tina
- Happiness becomes you
- Tina Turner, That's My Life
- Ich, Tina. Mein Leben
- Yo Tina
- My Love Story

Chapter 3: Facts About Tina Turner You Didn't Know

1. Tina Turner is not Her Real Name

Tina Turner was conceived as Anna Mae Bullock. She started her music profession with "Ike Turner's Lords of Beat" under the name "Little Ann" of which she showed up on her most memorable record, "Boxtop".

She appeared as Tina Turner in 1960 with the hit two part harmony single "A Blockhead in Affection". The pair became quite possibly the most considerable live demonstration ever". They delivered hits, for example, "It Will Turn Out Great", "Waterway Profound - Mountain High", "Glad Mary", and

"Nutbush City Cutoff points" prior to disbanding in 1976.

2. She was Abandoned by her Mother at the Age of 11

As small kids, Tina and her three sisters were isolated from them during The Second Great War. She went to live with her fatherly grandparents in Haywood District, Tennessee, in the US.

She was brought together with her folks after the conflict and the family moved to Knoxville. The family got back to Nutbush following two years to reside in the Flagg Woods people group, where she went to her Grade School.

Her mom deserted the family and moved to St. Louis, referring to her harmful relationship with her dad. Tina and her sisters were shipped off to live with their mother in Tennessee two years after the fact after her dad remarried.

3. She Started Singing in Nightclubs

She joined the band and turned into a highlighted entertainer performing with the band around St. Louis clubs. During this period, she took in the better marks of vocal control and execution.

Tina recorded her most memorable single "Boxtop" with the band in 1958. She was the main entertainer on the record close by Ike and individual Lords of Cadence artist Carlson Oliver.

4. She was a Founder Member of "Ike & Tina Turner Revue"

Tina Turner was brought into the universe of music with the single "A Bonehead In Adoration" which was acknowledged in July 1960. It came to No. 2 on the Hot R&B Sides outline and negative. 27 on the Bulletin Hot 100.

After the progress of her most memorable single, she and Ike made the "Ike and Tina Turner Revue". It incorporated the Lords of Beat and a young lady bunch, the Ikettes, as support entertainers and artists.

It became perhaps of the best pair throughout the entire existence of the US, delivering hits, for example, "It Will Turn Out Great", "Waterway Profound - Mountain High", "Pleased Mary", and

"Nutbush City Cutoff points" prior to disbanding in 1976.

5. She worked as a Domestic worker

As a teen, Tina filled in as a homegrown laborer for the Henderson family. She was at the Henderson house when she was told that her relative Evelyn had kicked the bucket in an auto collision close to her cousins Margaret and Vela Evans.

A self-purported fiery girl, Tina joined both the cheerleading crew and the female b-ball group at Carver Secondary School in Brownsville.

Tina went to live with her mom in St. Louis after her grandma passed on, where she moved on from Sumner Secondary School in 1958. She likewise functioned as a medical caretaker's helper at Barnes-Jewish Clinic.

6. Tina Turner Started went Solo in 1976

Later "Ike and Tina Turner Revue" disbanded in 1976, Tina began showing up on Television programs for the purpose of acquiring pay. She continued visiting to take care of her obligations with funds given to her by Joined Specialists chief Mike Stewart after Ike and Turner's gigs were dropped because of a claim.

In 1978, Turner delivered her third independent collection, Harsh, on Joined Craftsmen with dissemination in North America and Europe on EMI. That collection, alongside its 1979 development, Love Blast, which incorporated a short redirection to disco music, neglected to diagram, so Joined Specialists Records and Turner headed out in different directions.

7. Turner is a practicing Buddhist

Turner has once in a while alluded to herself as a "Buddhist — Baptist", implying her childhood in the Baptist church childhood where her dad was a Minister, and her later change to Buddhism as a grown-up.

In a 2016 meeting with Lion's Thunder magazine, she pronounced, "I see myself as a Buddhist." The February 15, 1979 issue of Fly magazine highlighted Turner with her Buddhist special stepped area on the cover.

8. She Suffered a Stroke

In 2013, three weeks after her wedding to Erwin Bach, Tina experienced a stroke and needed to figure out how to walk once more. In 2016, She was determined to have digestive malignant growth and picked homeopathic solutions for treating her hypertension which brought about harm to her kidneys and possible kidney disappointment.

Her possibilities of getting a kidney were low, and she was encouraged to begin dialysis. She thought about helping self destruction and joined to be an individual from Exit, yet Bach proposed to give a kidney for her transfer. Turner had a kidney replaced as a medical procedure on April 7, 2017.

9. She is a Mother and Grandmother

Turner had two natural children, Craig Raymond Turner and Ronald Renelle Turner, known as Ronnie. She likewise took on two of Ike Turner's kids, Ike Turner Jr. what's more, Michael Turner raising them as her own.

In July 2018, Craig Turner was found dead of a self-caused gunfire wound. Turner is a grandma of two.

10. She set the Guinness World Record

In 1988, Tina Turner visited the world for her 1986 collection, Defy Each Guideline. During her show in Rio De Janeiro, she set a then-Guinness Worldwide record for the biggest paying crowd for an independent entertainer, selling 180,000 tickets. This

41

presentation broke Straightforward Sinatra's 1980 record.

Printed in Great Britain
by Amazon